Reading and Writing Age 5–6

Rhona Whiteford

Rhona Whiteford has many years' experience of teaching at preschool and primary school level, and is the author of a wide range of educational books for teachers, parents and children. She has two children.

Consultant: **Andrew Burrell**

Andrew Burrell has worked as a primary school teacher and as a lecturer at the Institute of Education, University of London, and has carried out research into the teaching of Language and Literacy.

Illustrated by **Chantal Kees**

About this book

This book contains reading and writing activities suitable for 5- and 6-year-olds. They are based on the National Curriculum and National Literacy Strategy requirements for Year 1.

The activities gradually become more demanding, so it is important to start at the beginning.

The reading and writing activities taught or practised in each unit are stated at the top of the page. A note at the foot of the page tells you more about the purpose of the activities and gives advice about how to help your child with them.

'Superstar' stickers are included to help motivate children. There is a space for your child to stick a star when he or she has completed a unit. The 'Look what I have learned' page at the back of the book has space for another star, and is intended to give your child a sense of achievement, while providing you with a useful checklist of skills.

Each unit ends with a positive comment. Encouragement from you will work wonders, so be generous with your praise!

How to help your child

- Find a quiet place to work, preferably sitting at a table. Good posture helps the hand and arm to move freely.

- Work with your child little and often, but don't insist if he or she is tired or happily doing something else. Help with reading the instructions where necessary.

- Encourage your child to check his or her work.

- Read with or to your child every day. Use a variety of materials: comics, instructions, stories and rhymes.

- Look for things to read in your local environment: signs, notices, adverts and street names.

- Join a library and choose a book yourself. Experiment with your reading – children readily learn by example.

- Make opportunities for your child to write notes, messages and lists. Write a story together. Try to do some writing together every day.

Above all, be relaxed – and have fun!

*Hodder
Children's
Books*
a division of
Hodder Headline Limited

Matching words

My name is Hetty. I'm going to help you with your reading and writing.

Find the pairs of matching words.
Draw a line to join each pair.
Use a different colour for each line.

Write the words.
Learn them.

did	do
do	did
got	jump
jump	got
made	make
make	made
will	be
be	will

....

....

....

....

....

....

....

In Years 1 and 2, most children learn a list of 'school words' by sight, building on the words they learned in the Reception Year. The words in the activities on pages 2 and 3 are taken from that list. Help your child to look carefully at the words on this page and to memorise their shapes, drawing lines to join the identical words.

2

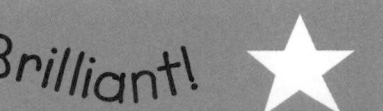

Brilliant!

Word starters

Look at the picture.
Say the word.
Find the word.
Complete the word.

Which sound does your name start with?

man	girl	house	water
door	bed	night	people

1 man..............

2 girl..............

3 door..............

4 b.ed..............

5 w.ater..............

 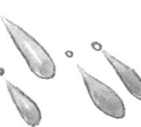
6 n.ight..............

7 ho.use..............

8 p.eople..............

Ask your child to name each picture and to say the school word, concentrating on the first sound. He should then find that word in the box, and copy it next to the picture.

Fantastic!

3

Labels

Look at the picture.
Find the word.
Write the label.

I've drawn a picture of the wolf from **Red Riding Hood!**

paw

leg

claw

nose

apron

tail

cap

1 nose

2 cap

3 paw

4 apron

5 tail

7 leg

6 claw

Hetty

Help your child to complete the labels neatly.

Look for labels in books and comics, and on food packaging and instructions for toys and games.

4

Well done!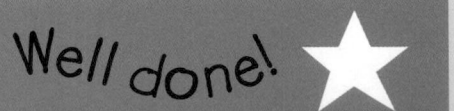

Captions

**Read the caption.
Complete the caption and
join it to its picture.**

cat	as
fast	at

Who is your favourite story character?

1 A .... runner

2 As white .... snow

3 A clever .... in clothes

4 Good .... climbing

Snow White

The Gingerbread Man

Jack and the Beanstalk

Puss in Boots

Talk about the pictures, and read the titles of these familiar stories together. Read each caption to your child, asking her to decide which of the possible answers works best in the space.

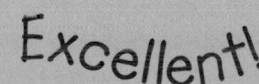

Excellent!

5

Sentences

A **sentence** is a short piece of writing that makes sense on its own.

Choose a word to complete the sentence. Draw a line under the word.

1.  I can | on | <u>see</u> | a boat.

2.  The girl | ~~his~~ | has | a ball.

3. 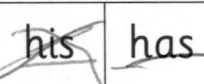 This is his | go | <u>house</u> | .

4.  Here are | this | <u>three</u> | dogs.

Now write the words here.

This activity gives your child the opportunity to practise reading and writing some school words.

Read each sentence together, and help your child to decide which word will make sense in the space.

Write the labels.
Write Yes if the piece of writing is a sentence.
Write No if it is not.

The two boys are laughing.

5 Yes

Molly hat big

This man happy

6 Yes

7 yes

Ben is an old dog.

8 YES

This is a happy Hetty!

Yes

Great! ★

7

Capital letters and full stops

Complete these book titles.

Goldilocks
Aladdin
Little Bo Beep
Cinderella
Bambi
Anansi
Tarzan

Remember that a name starts with a capital letter.

1  ☑ inderella

2 ☑ laddin

3 ☑ arzan

4 ☑ nansi

5 ☑ oldilocks

6 ☑ ittle ☑ o ☐ eep

7

Punctuation marks help to clarify the meaning of a piece of text, and children need to be shown how to use them correctly in their own writing. Point out to your child that the complete book titles can be found in the box.

A full stop shows you where the sentence finishes.

Hetty's friends have done some writing about their favourite food.

Tick each correctly written sentence. Write the others again.

 **8** I like carrots for tea.

 **9** i like sausages best

 **10** my favourite food is nuts

 **11** i like to eat Hetty's food.

A sentence begins with a capital letter and ends with a full stop. Point out these features when you are looking at books or your child's own writing together, and take a deep breath after each full stop to exaggerate the pause before the next sentence.

When you are assessing your child's work, check for sense and then for punctuation.

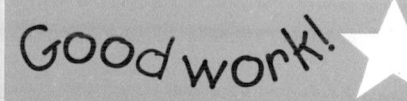

Listening for rhymes

Rhymes are words which sound similar.

Join the two rhyming words.
Write another rhyming word
in the balloon.

men

pen

1
cat
bat

2
jug

3
fin

mug

pin

4
ten
10

hen

5
hot

rot

Children who are taught to listen carefully to the sounds of words often become good at spelling. Help your child to read the words aloud, listening for rhymes and joining the pairs of rhyming words. There are a number of alternatives for the third rhyming word in each group.

Good!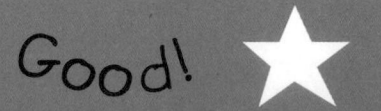

Picture rhymes

I'm a horse, of course!

Listen to the rhyme.
Say the word for each picture.

---

1. Mary, Mary, quite contrary,
   How does your garden grow?
   With cabbages,  and big black ,
   And a noisy big black !

---

2. Tom, Tom, the Piper's son
   Stole my and had some fun!
   But Ted chased Tommy down the street,
   As he had magic in his .

3. One, two, three, four, five,
   Once I caught a alive!
   Six, seven, eight, nine, ten,
   He jumped on a to get a .

   I gave him paper and ink, you know;
   He wrote a book on Mexico!

Children can memorise poems quite easily because of the rhythm and rhyme in the lines. This develops memory and concentration, and gives a sense of achievement. Not all the rhyming words on this page are spelled in a similar way, but this is purely a listening activity for your child.

Using picture clues to predict words is another important early reading skill.

Wonderful!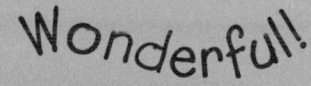

11

Talking about stories

When Little Red Riding Hood went to visit her grandmother she took a basket of cakes.

1 **What would you take on a visit to a friend or relative? What would you wear? Draw a picture.**

Jack sold his cow for a handful of beans!

2 **What would you buy? Draw a picture. Write two sentences about it.**

The activities on this page will help to develop your child's imagination in preparation for story writing. Discuss each of the two fairytales and your child's responses to the questions before she starts drawing and writing.

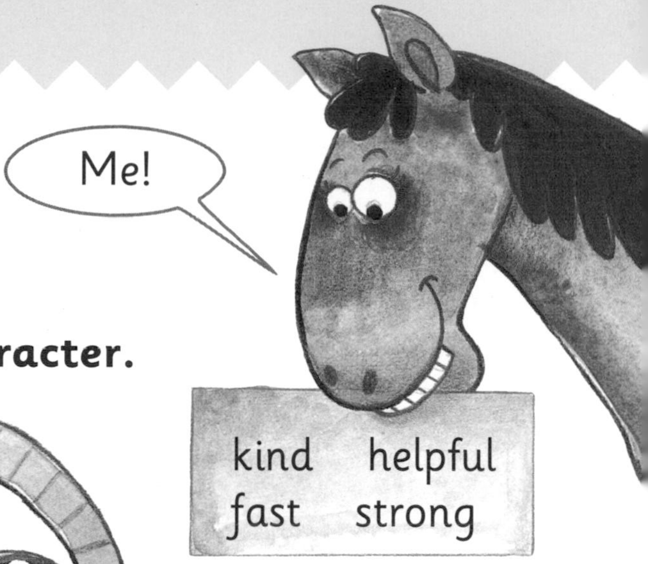
Me!
kind helpful
fast strong

3 **Listen to these describing words.**
Match each one to the correct character.

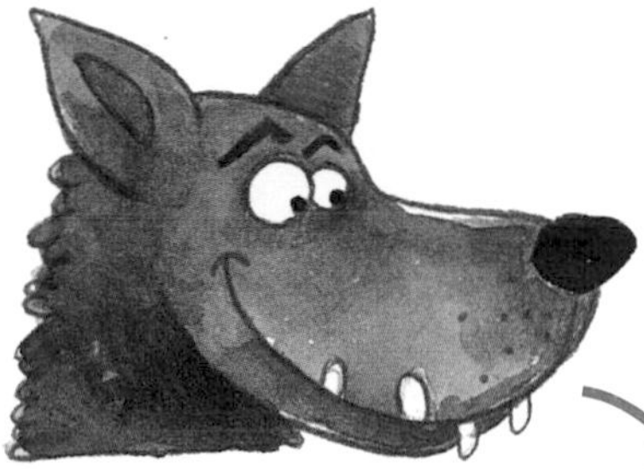

The wolf

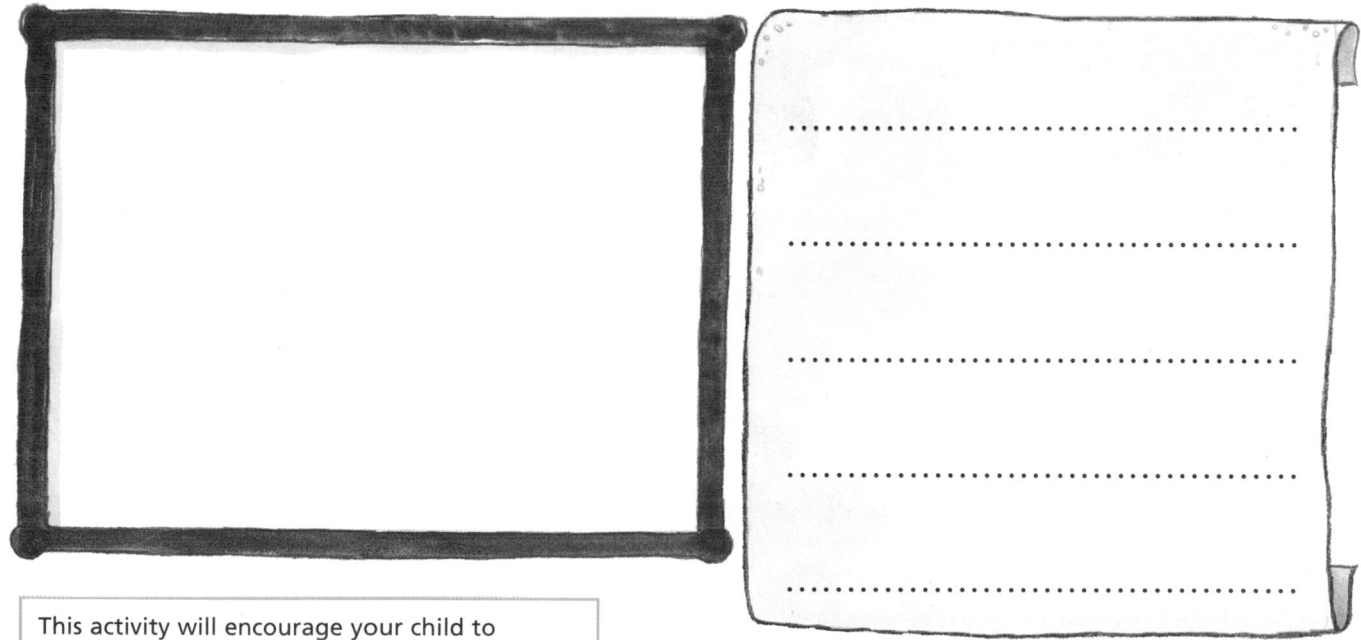

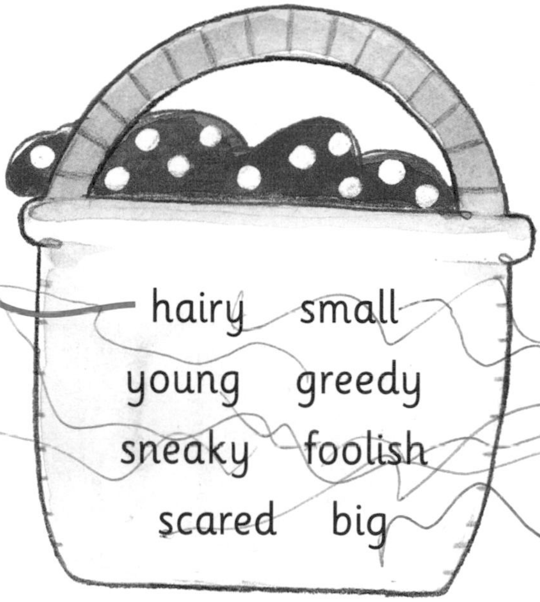
hairy small
young greedy
sneaky foolish
scared big

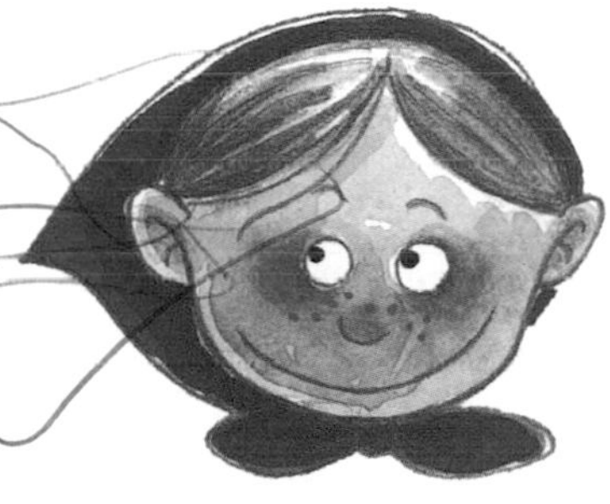

Red Riding Hood

4 **Who could you pretend to be?**
Draw yourself. Write some describing words.

This activity will encourage your child to concentrate on a task, and to develop her vocabulary. Discuss the characters and the describing words (adjectives), perhaps referring to other familiar story characters. Help your child with the writing activity.

Brilliant!

Talking about book covers

Find out about each of these books.

Look at the front and back covers.

Read the **title** and the **author's name**. Look at the **picture**. Read what is on the back **cover**.

A tale of magic and adventure that will make you laugh!

The Princess and the Knight

by B. Careful

This book is about

....

....

....

....

An easy guide to growing flowers

Summertime in the Garden

by A. Plant

This book is about

....

....

....

....

14

Read each book title and author's name to your child, and discuss the illustration on the front cover. Read the 'blurb', or description, on the back cover. Talk about the difference between fiction (stories) and non-fiction (factual text). Help your child to write a short sentence about the book.

Look at the covers of some real books together.

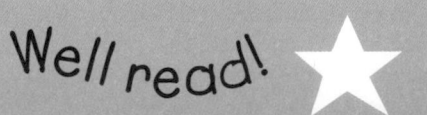

Well read!

Choosing books

This is **my** favourite book!

Black Beauty

A tale of a special horse

by Anna Sewell

**Listen to each question.
Write Yes or No.**

Do you like books?

Do you like stories?

Do you like non-fiction books?

Do you like books with pictures in them?

Do you like poems and rhymes?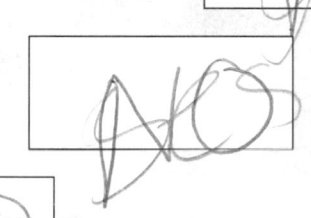

Do you like comics?

My three favourite books are

....

....

....

Children need to know that there are many different kinds of reading material. This activity will help your child to think about the range of texts available to him, and to begin to form his own tastes.

Fantastic!

15

Writing names

There is a present inside each parcel!
Guess what it is, and decide who to
give it to (a friend or relative).
Write his or her name on the parcel.

Hetty

Remember –
a name starts
with a **capital
letter**!

Look at the differently shaped parcels together, and
discuss what may be inside each one. Help your child to
decide on suitable recipients, and write their names clearly
in the school style on a sheet of paper for her to copy.

16

Good ideas!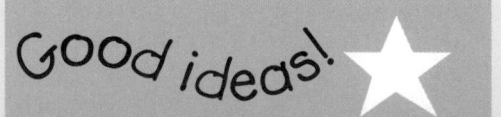

Questions

After a **sentence**, we write a **full stop**. .

After a **question**, we write a **question mark**. ?

Write some question marks.

What are they saying?
Complete each of these with a full stop
or a question mark.

1. I like you

2. How are you

3. I want to come with you

4. Where are you going

5. What is it

6. I like to eat grass and hay

This activity will help to develop your child's imagination. Read each speech aloud, using a suitable voice! Your intonation will help your child to decide whether or not a question is being asked.

Well done! ⭐

How many?

Sometimes we need to write the word for a number.

| one | 1 | three | 3 | five | 5 | seven | 7 | nine | 9 |
| two | 2 | four | 4 | six | 6 | eight | 8 | ten | 10 |

Write the number words.

1 ....two...... red roses

2 ......four...... knobbly noses

3 ......ten...... squirting hoses

4 ......three... giant locks

5 ......seven... huge rocks

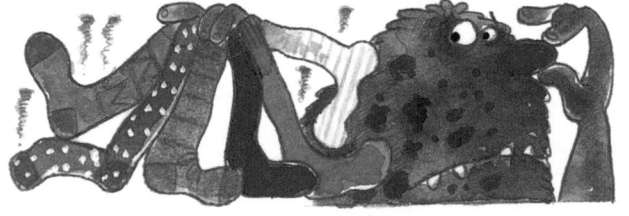

6 ......six........ smelly socks

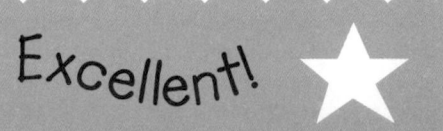

Excellent!

Your child will frequently meet number words in his reading, and it is important to be able to write them as well. Encourage your child to concentrate on learning a few number words at a time.

18

The days of the week

I'm Friday's child.

Here are the names of the days of the week.

Monday	Tuesday	Wednesday
Thursday	Friday	Saturday	Sunday

Complete this rhyme.

M.*onday*.........day's child has run a race,

T.*hursday*.day's child has a cheeky face,

I'm Monday's child. How about you?

W.*ednesday*.day's child is ready to go,

T.*uesday*.day's child is never slow,

F.*riday*....day's child likes laughing and living,

S.*aturday*..day's child is very forgiving,

But the child who is born on the seventh day

Is full of giggles and shouts "Hooray!"

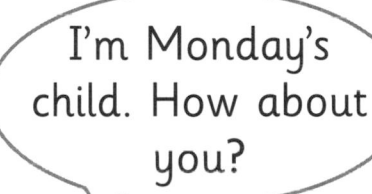

These are frequently used words, too. Point out the
initial capital letters, and write the words on card for
reading and writing practice. Write the original rhyme
(*Monday's child is fair of face*) on a sheet of paper,
leaving out the names of the days. Ask your child to
write them in the spaces.

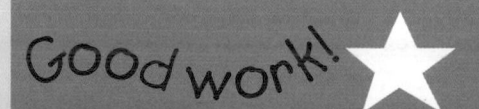

Good work!

19

School words

This is a good way of learning a new word!

Learn to read and write each of these school words.

Look at it...	Say it...	Cover it...	Write it...	✔ or ✗

Check it!

what	ist	
when	ist	
where	ist	
will		
with		
would		
want		

The words in this activity are high-frequency words which most children learn by sight in Years 1 and 2. Encourage your child to recognise them by shape rather than by sounding out the letters. She should practise writing them using the *Look, say, cover, write, check* strategy shown above.

20

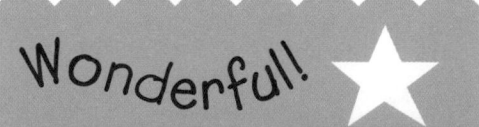

Wonderful!

The alphabet

h for **horse** comes before **i** and after **g**!

g | h | i

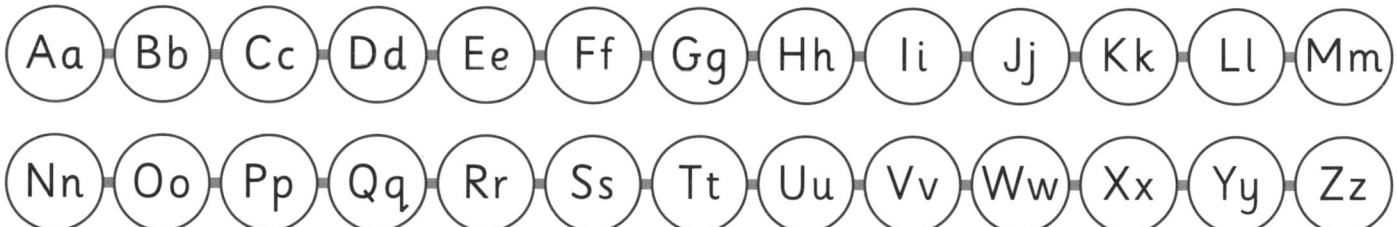

Aa – Bb – Cc – Dd – Ee – Ff – Gg – Hh – Ii – Jj – Kk – Ll – Mm

Nn – Oo – Pp – Qq – Rr – Ss – Tt – Uu – Vv – Ww – Xx – Yy – Zz

Write the missing letters.

1
| A | B | C | c | D | F | G | H |

2
| i |
| j |
| K |
| L |
| m |
| N |
| o |
| P |
| q |

3
| r |
| S |
| t |
| u |
| v |
| w |
| X |
| y |
| Z |

4 My favourite toys
(in alphabetical order)

....

....

....

....

....

Children need to know the order of the alphabet because information is often organised in alphabetical order. Help your child to find the missing letters (upper or lower case) by saying the alphabet with her.

Brilliant!

21

Listen and draw

I wonder what spiders eat.

**Listen to the poem.
Draw a picture.**

Sally Spider flew a glider.
Off she went each day,
With a metre of thread
And a hat on her head,
To explore the Milky Way.

She took a rug,
And a big blue jug
Which carried her food, you see.
An ant, a bug,
And a little green slug
Were all packed up for tea!

**Finish this note.
Show it to your helper.**

Please may I have

....

for my tea?

From ....

Read the poem two or three times to make sure your child has understood it and can draw the picture. Let him run his finger under the words as you read.

Fantastic! ★

What comes next?

Complete each instruction with one of these words.

When   First   Then   Finally   Next

Whoopee! Time for tea!

How to make Hetty's tea

1 First............... , get six carrots.

2 When............... you have done that, get a scoop of bran.

3 Next............... , we need a scoop of pony nuts.

4 Then............... you must mix all these things in my bowl.

Hetty

5 Finally............

Give it to me, please!

Instructions need to be written, and followed, in the correct sequence. Look at other sets of instructions (e.g. recipes, directions for using construction toys, rules for board games or computer games).

Well done! ★

Complete the story

Listen to the story. Write a word in each space.

Jungle trouble

It was hot and steamy in the jungle. Sir Samuel Saucepot was

trudging after [1]_____ wife, Lady Lily. She loved exploring,

and she wanted [2]_____ see every bit of the jungle.

After them trailed the little Saucepots, Sid, Sally [3]_____ Sue.

Each carried a huge pack containing food and water – and

[4]_____ , because they all loved reading.

Suddenly, [5]_____ heard a twig snap! Then came a

snuffling, and [6]_____ sniffling ...

What do you think will happen next?

Read the story to your child, running your finger along under the text and pausing slightly when you come to a space. Then read it again, stopping at the end of each sentence. Write the words for your child to copy.

Excellent!

Six stories

A story **setting** is the **place** where the story happens.

Here are descriptions of events from three fairytales. Can you name them?

1 A giant beanstalk grows up to the sky.

2 A biscuit runs away to escape being eaten.

3 A beautiful girl makes friends with an ugly beast.

**Look at each of these story settings.
List some events which could happen in each setting.**

4

man gergn Car

5

6

Talk about the pictures and make some suggestions for story events (things that happen), e.g. a robbery and a police chase, an accident and a rescue, getting lost on a picnic. Write your child's ideas on a sheet of paper for her to copy.

Good work!

More about stories

Draw a line to match each character to a setting.
Write a name for the character.

Discuss ways of linking the characters to the settings; there are no 'right answers'. Who are the characters? What have they been doing? What time of day is shown in each setting?

I'm a **good** character!

Listen to these describing words.

cowardly	sly	rough	strong	cruel	loving
cheerful	gentle	heroic	wicked	weak	kind

Draw two characters. Write a list of words for each one.

Good

Channelle

5 ....

6 .....chantelle........................

7 ....

8 ....

Bad

9 .....channelle...........................

10 .....chantelle...........................

11 ....

12 ....

This activity will develop your child's imagination and encourage him to concentrate on a task. The words in the box are suggestions only; others can be included.

Clever! ⭐

27

Who, when and where?

Write about an outing or a holiday.

I won a prize at a horse show!

Where did you go?	to the car
When?	Monday
Who else went?	
What happened first?	
What happened next?	
What happened in the end?	I went the car

Story writing and non-fiction writing may require your child to describe events in the correct sequence. Talk about a recent visit or activity, and help your child to write about the events in a logical order. Encourage her to write in complete sentences.

Wonderful!

Reading and writing at home

Do you have books in your home?

**Write the names of the people
who read these:**

Books ....

Newspapers ....

Comics ....

Letters ....

Write the names of the people who write these:

Notes ....

Letters ....

Lists ....

Cards ....

Who reads and writes most? ....

This activity will help your child to understand the
many purposes of reading and writing. Discuss the
questions fully, encouraging your child to give
thoughtful, honest answers.

Well done! ⭐

My own story

Make notes for your story here.

A story needs a **beginning**, a **middle** and an **ending**.

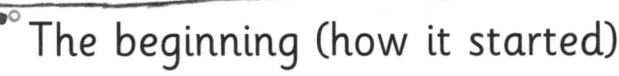

Characters	Setting	Time and weather

The beginning (how it started)

The middle (what happened)

The ending (how things were sorted out)

Stories are difficult to write, and good ones need to be planned carefully. Help your child to make brief notes in each box, drawing on ideas from previous pages if he wants to.

Brilliant!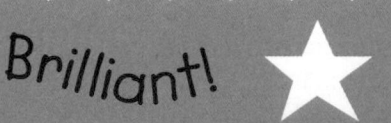

See what I can do

I can write a story!

My story is called [ ]

....

....

....

....

....

....

....

I enjoyed that!

Encourage your child to write his story independently, but show him how to refer back to the plan on page 30, and write words for him to copy if necessary. Let him read the story to you as he goes along, so that he can spot any inconsistencies.

Fantastic! ★

Answers

Page 2

Identical words should be linked by a line. Make sure that the words are correctly spelled.

Page 3

1 man 2 girl 3 door 4 bed
5 water 6 night 7 house
8 people

Page 4

1 nose 2 cap 3 paw 4 apron
5 tail 6 claw 7 leg

Page 5

1 fast 2 as 3 cat 4 at
Each caption should be linked by a line to its picture.

Pages 6–7

1 see 2 has 3 house 4 three
Make sure that the words are correctly spelled.
5 Yes 6 No 7 No 8 Yes

Pages 8–9

1 Cinderella 2 Aladdin 3 Tarzan
4 Anansi 5 Goldilocks
6 Little Bo Peep 7 Bambi
8 ✓ 9 I like sausages best.
10 My favourite food is nuts.
11 I like to eat Hetty's food.

Page 10

1 cat – bat – fat/hat/mat/pat/rat/
sat/vat
2 jug – mug – bug/dug/hug/lug/pug/
rug/tug
3 fin – pin – bin/din/kin/sin/tin/win
4 ten – hen – den/fen/men/pen/yen
5 hot – rot — cot/dot/got/jot/lot/
not/pot/tot

Page 11

1 bats cats crow
2 bear feet
3 bee chair pen

Pages 12–13

1 *Look for detail in the drawing.*
2 *Look for detail in the drawing, and check that the sentences make sense and are correctly punctuated.*

3 *The wolf*: hairy greedy
sneaky big
Red Riding Hood: small young
foolish scared
2 *Look for detail in the drawing, and check that the describing words suit the chosen character.*

Page 14

Your child's description of each book should be based on information learned from its cover.

Page 15

Look for honest, thoughtful answers.

Page 16

Make sure that the names are correctly spelled and that each one begins with a capital letter.

Page 17

1 I like you.
2 How are you?
3 I want to come with you.
4 Where are you going?
5 What is it?
6 I like to eat grass and hay.

Page 18

1 two 2 four 3 five 4 three
5 seven 6 six

Page 19

Make sure that the names of the days are correctly spelled.

Page 20

Make sure that the words are correctly spelled.

Page 21

1 –B–DE–G–
2 ––k l–n–p–
3 –s–u v–x–z
4 *Make sure that the toys are listed in alphabetical order.*

Page 22

Make sure the details in the picture match those in the poem.
Correct the spelling in the note if necessary.

Page 23

1 First 2 When 3 Next 4 Then
5 Finally

Page 24

1 his 2 to 3 and 4 books
5 they 6 a
Alternative answers are acceptable as long as they make sense in the sentences.

Page 25

1 Jack and the Beanstalk
2 The Gingerbread Man
3 Beauty and the Beast
4–6 *Check that the story ideas match the pictures.*

Pages 26–27

1–4 *Your child should make logical links between the characters and the settings, and suggest suitable names for the characters.*
5–8 *Any of the following*: strong loving cheerful gentle heroic kind (*alternative answers are acceptable*)
9–12 *Any of the following*: cowardly sly rough cruel wicked weak (*alternative answers are acceptable*)

Page 28

Check that the facts are in the correct order, and that the sentences are correctly written.

Page 29

Look for thoughtful answers, and make sure that capital letters have been used to begin names.

Pages 30–31

Look for imaginative ideas with plenty of detail, and make sure that the notes are in the correct boxes. Check that the story follows the story plan. Look for complete sentences, correctly spelled and punctuated.